Inside My Mind

Other books by Steven Darter

Lessons From Life: Four Keys to Living with More Meaning, Purpose, and Success

Managing Yourself, Managing Others: Learn How to Improve Effectiveness, Productivity, and Work Satisfaction

"I have been a fan of Steve Darter's writing for many years, so this collection of poems comes as no surprise to me. *Inside My Mind* delves deep into the human experience. Steve's reflective and poignant poetry captures the essence of life's profound moments, weaving together themes of love, loss, aging, and spirituality with remarkable clarity and emotional depth. His poems on family, relationships, and personal growth resonate with authenticity and wisdom, making them relatable to readers from all walks of life. This is more than just a collection of poems; it is a testament to the resilience of the human spirit and the enduring power of faith and love. Steve's heartfelt and thought-provoking poetry will leave a lasting impact on your soul. You might be surprised at how these poems resonate with you."

—**TOMMY THOMAS**, founder, JobfitMatters; author of *The Perfect Search*; speaker; podcast host, Next Gen Nonprofit Leadership with Tommy Thomas

"Steve Darter's poetic journey brilliantly reflects on, and expresses, a full array of emotions, both disturbing and beautiful, most of which we all experience over the course of our human lives. Take it all in if you dare. They are pivotal inspirational revelations worth waiting for."

—**FRED SIEVERT**, author of *God Revealed* and *Grace Revealed*; retired president of a Fortune 100 corporation

"*Inside My Mind* offers poems on a wide span of topics covering all the stages of life's journey. The reader will find expressions of the highs and lows of life experiences, from the heights of joy and peace to the depths of hopelessness and despair. One is drawn to gratitude for the blessings given along the way, as well as for the support received during times of intense struggle. I finished these poems with a strong desire to share them with family, friends, persons in acute emotional pain and others welcoming newfound joy. Thank you, Steve, for putting these emotional expressions in print."

—**MARGARET CROWLEY**, retired educator and designer of several leadership, education, and elder care programs

"Steve Darter's new poetry collection, *Inside My Mind*, gathers together thoughtful quiet moments of introspection as he reflects on life's biggest challenges and transitions. These poems offer a powerful testament to the resilience of the human spirit. Darter's words serve as a compassionate guide, illuminating the path through darker times with glimmers of hope, love, and the eternal nature of growth and transformation."

—**ROBERT REX WALLER** Jr., associate professor of writing and director, USC Writing Center, The Writing Program, University of Southern California; singer-songwriter and lead singer for the critically acclaimed roots band, "I See Hawks in L.A."

"'Do You Remember Me?' is the title for one of Darter's poems addressed to his father. One can say that Darter's debut collection is a way he remembers himself to himself and to fortunate readers. He fulfills Wilde's words: Memory is the diary we all carry about with us. This collection is a diary of days from youth to aging years, with poems that are passionate without sentimentality, reflective minus arrogance, and indeed have a mirth, fueled by an ongoing gratitude to have lived, and to live."

—**NANCY ANNE MILLER**, Bermudian poet; author of eleven poetry books and *Selected Poems*, forthcoming from Valley Press

"*Inside My Mind* is an extraordinary collection of ninety-five poems that touch the heart and soul. Each one is a profound reflection on life's journey, offering deep insights and moving experiences. I can attest to the brilliance of this work—it may be his best book yet. A must-read for anyone seeking wisdom and inspiration."

—**BLAINE GREENFIELD**, CEO, BLAINESWORLD; author of four books, including *75 Quotes for 75 Years*

Inside My Mind

Thought-Provoking Poems about Love, Life,
People, Aging, Moving On, and God

Steven M. Darter

RESOURCE *Publications* • Eugene, Oregon

INSIDE MY MIND

Thought-Provoking Poems about Love, Life, People, Aging, Moving On, and God

Copyright © 2024 Steven M. Darter. All rights reserved. Except for brief quotations in critical publications or reviews, no part of this book may be reproduced in any manner without prior written permission from the publisher. Write: Permissions, Wipf and Stock Publishers, 199 W. 8th Ave., Suite 3, Eugene, OR 97401.

Resource Publications
An Imprint of Wipf and Stock Publishers
199 W. 8th Ave., Suite 3
Eugene, OR 97401

www.wipfandstock.com

PAPERBACK ISBN: 979-8-3852-2591-0
HARDCOVER ISBN: 979-8-3852-2592-7
EBOOK ISBN: 979-8-3852-2593-4
VERSION NUMBER 07/19/24

To my wife, Diane, who for fifty-two years has put up with my intense and at times erratic ways; my granddaughter, Libby, whose poetry inspired me to write this book; my children, Kevin and Katie and grandson, David who allow me to be part of their lives; the people I've met and interviewed, whose stories have enriched me beyond belief; and God who made me who I am and without Him none of this would have been possible.

Contents

Continual Learning | 1

Awakening Myself | 2

Love of Family

If You're Lucky Enough | 5
You are...... | 7
A Loving Marriage is ... | 9
With Her | 10
Getting Home | 11
Say It | 11
Waking Up | 11
Unconscious Beauty | 12
Impending Fatherhood | 13
A Lost Child | 14
What Could Be | 17
To My Daughter | 19

To My Grandson | 20
There is No Greater Gift | 22
Finding Treasure | 23
Being There | 25
Mom | 27
Visiting My Father | 29
Do You Remember Me? | 31
A Moment Between Father and Son | 33
Upon My Father's Death | 37
Without Relationships | 41

Observing People

Stagnation | 45
Like Jonathan Livingston Seagull | 46
Suppression is Oppression | 47
Their Relationship | 49
Drugs | 50
Depravity | 51
Elusively Present | 53
He's Afraid | 55
Remember That Place? | 56
Listening | 58
Over the Edge, into the Abyss | 59
Another Casualty | 60

I had No Answer | 61
Fate | 63
Trying to Recover | 64
Trapped | 65
His Changing State of Mind | 66
What is He Becoming? | 68
Lost Soul | 69
Loneliness | 70
You had the Power | 71
Saint Nancy | 73
Captain John | 75
Sigmund Freud | 78

Skippy | 79
The Counselor | 80
Temporary Reprieve | 81
Self-Abasement | 82
Freeing Himself | 83
Waiting Hopelessly | 85
Undue Influence | 86
Spiraling Downward | 88
Politicians at Their Worst | 90
Charisma | 91
Is It His Time? | 92
An Idea | 93
The End | 94
Suffering a Loss | 94

Burden | 95
Misplaced Anger | 96
Alone in Sadness | 97
Now It's Real | 98
Happiness | 99
Remnants from an Acid Trip | 100
Thoughts of Suicide | 101
Returning Home | 102
Social Anxiety | 103
Being Self-Conscious | 104
His Mind | 105
Perfection | 106
Hesitancy | 107

Approaching the End of Life on Earth

Approaching the End | 111
Coming to Terms with
  What Will Be | 113
Thoughts of Dying | 114
What's Comes Next | 115

Sleep Used to Be | 116
Sleep Now | 117
As the Door Slowly Closes | 120
One View of Death | 121

Moving On

Moving on from Loneliness | 125
Don't Give Up | 126
A Protective Wall | 127

We Can | 129
Momentum | 131

God

Spending Time with God | 135
There Comes a Time | 137
Always There | 139

Naivete | 140
He Is | 141
Feeling Connected | 142

Acknowledgments | 143
About the Author | 145

I'm seventy-five years old. Like many of you, I've observed, lived through, and experienced a lot. At times, life has ripped at my insides and other times it has been pure joy. During my professional career, I interviewed and evaluated close to five thousand people. Between climbing into the lives of others and living my own, I learned that hope and faith can prevail no matter how bad things may look, feel, and seem.

    I hope you find my poems thought-provoking, possibly helpful, hopefully not discouraging. Some I'm sure you'll relate to. Others, maybe not so much.

Continual Learning

Drifting,
In and out of myself,
Like the tide
Scratching at the surface
Of sand on a beach
My mind
My emotions

The process never ends,
This scratching away—
Coming and going
In and out
Discovering
With every claw
Learning,
From every stroke
Who I am
What I am meant to be
Why I am here
And the purpose of my life

Awakening Myself

My body—sagging
Pen—growing heavy
Heart—slowing down
Papers lying before me
Scribbled upon
Strewn about the room
Waiting to be collected and read
Written furiously
Felt intensely

In solitude
Awakening myself
With my own words

Love of Family

If You're Lucky Enough

If you're lucky enough to find someone
Who will love you,
Encourage you,
Respect you,
Support you,
Uplift you,
And fill in those parts for you
That have not been complete—
To help you become more of who you are and
Are meant to be,
Consider yourself lucky.

If you're lucky enough to find someone
Who will spend their life devoted to you and
A life fulfilled,
Cherish that person
Never let things big or small stand in the way
Of the beauty of that relationship

Hold hands whenever you can
Look at each other—
Really look at each other whenever you can
Be together, treasure every minute and moment
Devote yourself to each other

Grow the relationship
Appreciate it
Watch it evolve, change, strengthen, expand

Wake up every morning and see the wonder and beauty—Never lose it
Don't allow the oppression,
The frustrations,
The temptations of life
Or your insecurities or stubbornness
To destroy what you have
Dwell on what is positive, not what is negative
Wake up every morning and go to sleep each night
And say thank you
Thank you to God for allowing such beauty to exist
Thank you to each other for being there in your life
By your side, as your friend, as your lover, as your partner

You are. . . . . .

You are the light I see each day
The air I breathe
The sun that warms
The ocean I swim in
The scent of a flower that wafts
The summit I climb
The view that inspires
The motivation that compels
The touch I need
The smile that reassures
The laugh that makes all the bad disappear,
Even if only for a few seconds
The reassurance that consoles

That special moment we share
When we turn and look
And know,
In sync, together
Merged in spirit, in thought, in a feeling, in that moment
Whether it be happiness, sadness, joy, anger
Excitement, wonder, anticipation, delight
Grief, satisfaction, affection, passion, or pride
The range is endless

You are my love
My partner
The reason I am healthy, happy, alive
I am so grateful,
To God,
That he sent you into my life when I was adrift, unmoored
When there was no purpose, no reason
And I saw you, and I knew
I really did
Deep inside
Like light to darkness
A flame to a candle
Water to a parched soul

At that moment you became my existence
My reason to go on when all felt so lost
A way to live, a journey, an adventure
Together, hand-in-hand, as our lives merged
Wow!!

A Loving Marriage is . . .

A glow that never stops shining
A flame that never extinguishes
A warmth that never stops enveloping
A comfort that never goes away

A life so entwined,
Where both are stronger and weaker
Depending on each other
Over and over
Becoming one

Each separate
Distinct
Bringing uniqueness
Finding points of connectivity
Commonality
Appreciation
Respect
A life together
Enduring
Despite the pitfalls

With Her

Without her, I stand alone,
Cautiously—hesitantly approaching the world
An unsure conqueror—
Fearful of fear, loneliness,
Not belonging or connecting to anyone, any place, or anything

With her, my strength erupts
That internal will to win, move forward,
Succeed in a world of traps, challenges, tests of all kinds
With her, I am a conqueror of me.

With her, is comfort, a resting place
A haven to relax, recoup, grow stronger
With her, is a touch, a look, a smile, a friend, a home
Where I am anchored, grounded, connected
Where I feel alive—
Giving my life meaning and purpose
A place from which to venture out into the world
Enabling me to overcome and persist
Feeding an innate need for belonging

When I didn't have her,
My life felt like endless wandering,
Like a lost soul looking for its resting place

Getting Home

When you enjoy someone's company
As much as I do yours
You can't wait to fly home
To be in their arms

Say It

I couldn't say enough times
That I love you
Because if I lost you tomorrow
I would feel that I had not said it enough

Waking Up

Hearing you
Quietly preparing for the day
The rustling as you struggle
To leave the warmth of bed
The silent movements
Through early morning darkness
Feeling your presence
Slowly I stir
Shielding my eyes from the morning sun
Resting them on you

Unconscious Beauty

Your body
Turned gently last night
And in its wondrous slumber
Gracefully seeking my presence,
Your head rested on my shoulder
Your arm upon my chest
And your leg next to mine.

In the beauty of your sleep
You kissed my cheek
And said,
I love you

Impending Fatherhood

As a child, I would escape into a forest
Walking where others had not walked
Standing where no others stood
Dreaming of days to come
Where I could change the world

Capturing some moment in history
Wanting to be remembered
By someone for something

Now, all I want is to be remembered
By a child
Hoping I deserve
His love

A Lost Child

It wasn't so long ago
That we were in flight
To an oasis
In the middle of nowhere
To a final goodbye
Or a remarkable rebirth.
I prayed for the latter
But believed otherwise

I cried,
As the finality of this choice,
And path
Overwhelmed—
And carried home
With me
The reality
Of a lost son.

So beautiful at birth and
Energetic in youth
Gave way to terror,
Sadness,
And pain.

Who could have imagined this day
And more to come.
Who could have imagined
This son
Who was once so lost
To be found
To have found himself.
Who could have imagined
Anger, turned to understanding
Weakness to strength
Fear to Confidence
Grief to joy.
To imagine this day was
An impossible dream.

But there you were
Sitting on a bluff
In the middle of nowhere
Reflecting on your life
Watching an eagle soar.
How beautiful an image
How majestic
How fitting
How prophetic

You are about to set flight
On a path
Clear-headed
Confident—
You have become that eagle.

Who could have imagined
This graduation day,
What seemed so impossible
This outcome.

The pride
And love we feel
For our son
Who was, and is
So beautiful and energetic

Take flight,
Spread your wings
Today, you become a man.

What Could Be

All I have ever wanted
Is for you to be happy and successful.
To feel the flow—The glow of success.
To see you reach inside
To discover and realize
The potential I see in you

I see things you do and don't do
Mistakes you keep making
The instinct is to help you control
And manage the monster inside
Learn, grow
Develop, change
To teach as fathers should.

My father used to tell me over and over
In argument after argument:
If I didn't love you, I wouldn't care.
I'd huff and puff and walk away.
But I remember those words—even to this day.

He knew I could be more
Continually challenging me to be so.
Never giving up on me—

Even when I was at my worst.
Once he belted me in the jaw,
Knocking me to the ground—I deserved it.

I have never given up on you—never did.
Painful if I did—painful if I didn't
But now, I see glimmers of change, of hope—
Like a butterfly emerging from a caterpillar
A metamorphosis
From what is to what could be

To My Daughter

I held you in my arms
When you were born
You grabbed hold of my finger and squeezed
You slept on my chest
As I rocked you to sleep
I carried you down steps
Taught you to ride a bike and
How to throw a baseball
I watched as you crawled about the room
Walked out the door
Rode your bike down the street
Drove off to college
Moved away to take your first job
As you set up your own home

Sometimes,
I gave you advice
Sometimes,
I implanted a thought
Mostly,
I watched as you made wise choices
Without much help from me.
I have been with you always and
Have watched as your life unfolded and
This, my sweet daughter,
Has been your wonderful gift to me

To My Grandson

The day you were born
The moment I saw you
Held you in my arms
Your eyes singularly focused in wonderment
Latching onto mine

As I gazed at your
Tiny toes
Tiny hands
Tiny fingers
Delicate nose
Round cheeks
As I watched your mouth curl
Felt your movements—
Some so slight.
Listening,
To your steady breathing, coos, cries, sneezes, yawns

As I held you in my arms
Transported into another world
Feeling instant love
I knew that a special bond would emerge.

Grandfather and Grandson
Our special relationship
Hanging out—like friends
Talking, walking, exploring
(running between the raindrops)
Adventure stories I made up, we made up
Stories I told about my life,
My parents, grandparents, family history
Playgrounds, books we read, puzzles we did,
Games we played
Lovingly competing, always teasing, always laughing
Baseball, soccer, football, basketball, golf
And so much more

As you move through life
Fulfilling your dreams
Know that those moments with you
Makes my heart soar—a feeling that is hard to ignore
And will be with me forevermore

There is No Greater Gift

Her thoughts are deep
Her words flow
Pouring onto paper
Capturing a thought
A feeling
An observation
Illuminating
What's in her mind
In her heart
In her soul

She's a wonder to behold
Beautiful inside and out
How glorious it is
Watching her grow
Develop
Become
Who
She is destined to be

There is no greater gift
God can give
A grandfather
Than a granddaughter
like Libby

Finding Treasure

I loved telling stories
To my grandkids
About taking flight
About discoveries
Victories
Possibilities
Doing right

On a dragon we'd fly
Together, in search of treasure
Enemies we'd fight
Much to their delight
To the rescue, we'd come
Not to be outdone

As they got older, they'd take over
Setting them free to join me
Letting our imaginations loose
Producing stories that wowed
Making me proud
Of them
As we created gem after gem

Good memories like these
Are hard to contain
Forever they remain,
Within me,
As you can see by what I write—what I highlight
Like sunlight, oh so bright
To be involved
To be loved
What a pleasure;
I found the treasure

Being There

You weren't always the son we wanted.
You were a delight as a small child.
Winning us over quickly with your energy and smile.
You were a hellion as a teenager and
For a time, as an adult,
There was more grief than our hearts could bear.
But you turned it around.
Going beyond what a parent could want or expect.

You were there day in and day out.
Looking out for us, taking care of us, loving us
In a way that no one ever could.

You made our life at the end so much easier,
With your caring
Your smile
Your jokes
Your teasing
Your loving nature
Fighting for us—never once a complaint.

You were the son we needed as we declined.
When we could no longer care for ourselves.

Our spirits will forever be linked.
Thank you for being there, for us.
Love,
Mom and Dad
As we look down at you,
From Heaven

(Dedicated to my Brother Jay Barry Darter
who took care of our parents as they aged)

Mom

I have never seen eyes as sparkling as yours and
I don't think I ever will again.
A smile so inviting
A heart so loving
A spirit so touching

You taught me to love,
To appreciate,
To stop and listen to the water,
To look at the trees and sky,
The wonders of the beauty around us,
And what is in the heart and soul.

You were an adventure in and of yourself.
An artist and an explorer
Who, above all else, loved to touch people.

You could,
By who you were,
Reach inside anyone and
Get them to feel good about themselves.
You had an innocence about you,
That was so unique and wonderful.
You were a joy to be around.

You never lost who you were born to be—
This gift you had with people,
To touch their hand,
Smile, listen, and bring out in them
Feelings of warmth, love, importance, and value—
That may have been forgotten
Or, buried deep inside.

Mom, you have been God's light on this earth, and,
You are heading home.
To rejoin the great loves of your life.
They are all waiting to embrace you
To again feel joy from your presence.
But know, your loving eyes and smile,
And beautiful spirit will live in our hearts—forever

Visiting My Father

So often,
You seemed unappreciated
Unnoticed,
Not there,
Except for a few memories.

Your hands,
Trembling now,
Calloused by many years of labor
That made your body firm
Are but symbols.

The fatigue,
Sitting upon your face,
Echoing hardships
Is a scar of your working life.

A glimmer,
Resting in your eyes
Catches fire,
That spark in your soul,
From days you suffered most
And survived.

Your voice,
Often exploding in anger,
Reflecting hurts and haunts,
A final fighting of past images.

But mostly, I see the smile
That proudly warms the room
As you greet me at the door.

Do You Remember Me?

Not long ago
My boyish appearance
And pimply skin would burst into the room
With gales of happiness
Or cries of sadness.
How you comforted me then
Told me of a day
That was to be.
How hopeful of the future I became
And so silently scared of the next day.

Do you remember?
How, in my struggling age of independence,
We argued
Far into the night.
How I felt my wisdom was that
Of an experienced man,
And you knew it wasn't.

And now, do you see
How I've grown
To be the man
You knew I was meant to be.
To be able
To look at me

And see how much I've learned since then.
To be
As wise as I am now.
And to realize
How infinitely much more
I need to know
To be as wise as you were,
In raising me the way you did.

A Moment Between Father and Son

There I was
All of ten
Standing alone—
In the rain
Baseball glove in hand
Hat crooked
Tilted slightly to the side
Uniform too large
For my small frame
Looking up at the sky
Hoping, believing the rain would stop—
The game would be played.

I walked the half-mile
From my home
To the ballfield
In a downpour
Finally,
The rain was letting up,
Somewhat

I was alone
My parents worked that day
Into the evening

On my own
As I often was
Making decisions
Taking actions
Using what limited judgment I had

No one showed up
No coaches
No players
No parents
No umpires

I stood there
For a long time
Waiting
Near the chain-link fence
Close to home plate
Knowing the rain would stop
Knowing the game would be played
A car stopped
A man with an umbrella dashed out
Approached
Asked if I needed help

I explained,
There is a Little League game tonight
He smiled and said,
Son, I don't think so.
The game is rained out
A lump grew in my throat

Do you want a ride home?
No, the rain will stop, and we'll play.

He shook his head
Smiled
Walked briskly back to his car
Drove off

Again,
I was alone
Hoping the rain would stop
Hoping others would show up
Hoping to play the game

When darkness descended
I realized the truth
No matter how badly I wanted to play
I couldn't will it to happen

I arrived home
Drenched
There was my dad
Sitting in his chair
Tired from his long workday
As he often was,
Reading the newspaper.
He looked up
To see my sadness
Responding

He told me of his dream
To be a professional baseball player
How he was hired by a bank
At nineteen years of age
To be their pitcher
In a league of bank-sponsored baseball teams.

I knew the story
Heard it many times
Even though I was only ten

He told me
Of his disappointment
Not making it to professional baseball
To play for his beloved Yankees
How the bank closed suddenly
Overnight
As the Great Depression began—
Taking his job and dream away
How he found another job
As a butcher
Life goes on

He then hugged me close
Whispering,
I understand,
Communicating that
He felt my disappointment
My sadness
My pain

Upon My Father's Death

I stood there
Looking at my father
Numb, tears rolling down my face
Telling him I loved him.
A blanket,
Pulled up to his neck.

I touched his shoulder,
His cheek
Like he was sleeping.
I wanted to stay and also leave
What is the protocol?
I didn't know
So, I just talked to him.
Words flooded out.
I don't know what I said.

I stood there
Talking to him
Maybe for an hour
Maybe just a minute
I really don't know.
It all seemed to happen
In slow motion

My senses were sharp,
Singularly focused on the moment—on him,
The stubble on his face,
Off-white color of the blanket,
Pattern on the curtain pulled around the bed,
Muffled sounds from the hall,
The gray chair—in the corner,
Photos on the bookshelf,
The nebulizer.
He was very frail
lying there
The blanket pulled up to his neck.

The night before,
I held his hand.
He was fading in and out.
His eyes were closed.
Suddenly, he opened them and made a joke.
What a glorious moment.
Then he closed them.
Mom was there,
Holding one hand
And I the other.

Now he was no more.
At that moment
I didn't realize what is meant by the phrase
'Someone you love never leaves you
and is always in your heart.'
At that moment
It was all about sadness, loss, and the finality of death.
I had to tell my mother that her husband was no more.
They were married for seventy-two years.

The nurses had moved my mother into the hallway.
She was sitting there, alone,
Barely able to see,
Listening to the sounds and people around her.
She was not aware that Dad was dead

I sat next to her,
Took her hand into mine,
Stroked her face and hair, and
Told her that Dad had died.
I don't recall her immediate reaction.
We sat in silence, and then,
Instinctively, I knew
We had to go to a place
That would bring her comfort

We left the nursing home.
Drove to a nearby beach.
The setting was perfect.
Mom loved the beach—
The sand,
The water,
The smell of salt in the air,
And the sounds.
She was a nature lover.
Despite her limited eyesight,
The beach was a welcome assault on her senses.
She was in her comfort zone.

As we drove,
We talked.
At the beach,
I put her in a wheelchair.

We walked along the boardwalk and paths
and talked.
We stopped,
Looked out at the water and talked.
We had ice cream sodas,
And talked some more.
We laughed a lot.
We cried.
She remembered.
We connected—in a deep way.

She reminisced—about Dad.
How they met
Saw each other
He wearing a purple suit
With a big, floppy hat.

She told me about his look,
How he raised his eyebrows
Cary Grant style,
Gave her a smile,
Bolted from a chair,
Walked beside her.
Charmed his way into her heart.

Mom and I got through that day, and
I have not been the same since.

Without Relationships

Without someone
To share your accomplishments with
Feel your joy with
Be awed by beauty with
To smile with
Cry with
Touch

Without that person
Those people
Without relationships
There is an emptiness,
A void
Standing alone in a harsh world

Relationships we invest in
Whether they be family or friend
Nurture
Cherish
Acknowledge our existence,
Giving meaning
To our lives

Without them
Life would be hollow,
Incomplete

Observing People

Stagnation

Waiting,
Lying there—stuck
Reflecting on what was, what is, what could be

Waiting,
For the inevitable
For the next moment—maybe the last

Waiting,
For the next step
A new door
Whenever it will come
Whatever it will be
Wherever it will lead

Waiting,
For the unknown to reveal itself
With hope
With Prayer
Wondering, imagining, dreaming

Incredibly calm
Incredibly anxious
He waits,
For a fresh start, a new birth, a new journey
For this stagnant feeling to end

Like Jonathan Livingston Seagull

He's invisible on a beach
Toeing the sand
Penetrating his mind

Like the gull above
He dives and dips
Turns and twists
Seeking a source of life.

Like Jonathan,
He needs more than morsels of food.
Like Jonathan,
He needs to fly,
To spread his wings
And dive into the depths
Of the unanswered caverns of his mind.

Like Jonathan,
He'll take the plunge
And hope to rise in time.

Suppression is Oppression

Suppression is oppression
Whether self-inflicted or by others
Intentionally or unintentionally

Holding himself back
Not doing what God created him to do
Not being who God created him to be
Diminishing his life and God's intent

He needs to have faith, strength
To rise above the suppression
To overcome the oppression

It's not easy
He knows this—
He says—
A fight he faces each day
Periodically losing
Holding back out of fear
Suppressing himself
Oppressing himself
Lacking the confidence to move forward

He wishes he had a person, a team
That believed in him
That would step in, lift him up
When his knees grow weak
And his legs give out

Their Relationship

He said
She said
They said
Telling
Saying
Not listening
Not understanding
Not accepting
Anger exploding
Morphing into silent rage

Each going about
Their separate ways
Until calm arrives
Sometimes taking days

Their relationship is like waves
Rolling in, crashing
Doing damage
Returning to the ocean
Only to come back again
Majestic
Irresistible
Compelling
Occasionally destructive

Drugs

A candle,
Flickering shadows on a bare wall
Creating magnified illusions—
His presence is unnoticed

A needle,
Moving steadily across a disk
Producing the occasional crackling
Of a record in need of changing—
His footsteps are unheard

A cloud of smoke,
Searching for an open window
Stagnating the room
And a lamp
Hanging by its chord
In need of straightening
His voice sinks to the floor—ignored

The room has a stillness
Quietly absorbing the breaths of the occupants
Staring at reflections on walls
And in their minds
Unaware of each other
And possibly themselves
No one sees him leave

Depravity

It wasn't long ago
They waited in an alley for you
Coldness had swept in
They were out of cigarettes
In a strange place
Darkness kept them company

They waited like hungry dogs for dinner
Waited,
Till you walked by
Waited,
Although their anticipation rose
They waited

You looked around
Collar up
Hat pulled low
Face concealed
Eyes wide and black
They waited

You glanced their way
Nodded
Slipped into a door
They followed

They never saw your face
Didn't think it mattered
They were young—naïve—unaware

It wasn't long ago
When their bodies were dumped
In front of a hospital
It really wasn't very long ago

Elusively Present

She's there,
But seemingly not present,
Elusively gone
To where or what holds her back.

No explanation,
Just a faint smile.
A sort of acknowledgment,
But even that is elusive.

He rocks between
Anger
Frustration
Sadness
Emotional pain
To caring
Worry
Empathy
As he attempts to understand.

But understanding doesn't come.
There is,
No explanation
No dialog

No resolution
Just blankness
A hollowing out of what once was.

He's Afraid

He's afraid of being accused, abused, laughed at, rejected
He wishes he had the courage to take her in his arms
Hold her, caress her, love her
But he's afraid

He hides behind books, magazines, closed doors
He avoids her presence, her look, her touch
The comfort of her love

He's afraid to show her
To take the first step
So, he drifts further and further away
Waiting, hoping, watching, crying
Dreaming of better times

He's afraid, lonely, and needs her help
He says to himself,
Rescue me, please

Remember That Place?

It was easy to get there
Through a look, a touch, a thought
A memory, a possibility, a longing, a moment
Energy flowed
The spirit filled
Each day was a blessing
Life was great
Meaning and purpose always within grasp

They couldn't wait
They appreciated
Their eyes saw life at its fullest
Their hearts filled with joy, bliss, excitement
They remembered

They wished they knew the path back
It didn't seem out of reach
The desire was there
But their wills were lacking

Beneath the surface
Affecting it all was disappointment
Turned to anger
Not the raging type
That explodes and blinds

But the smoldering type
That is easy to accept and live with
Because it grows so slowly
Over time
Not addressed
Not talked about
Allowed to burn

Listening

They screamed at one another
Each taking a turn
One yelling traitor
The other yelling burn

They didn't need to know
What the other had meant
For truth rested solely
On what each had to vent

They pointed fingers
Raised their hands
And let emotions fly
The rock and gun
Replaced the word
And now we ask why

If I re…mem…ber,
He said
I can't seem to remember
What was in his head
But I was right
And that's for sure
Even if I can't remember
What we argued for.

Over the Edge, into the Abyss

He is a ruler with no kingdom
Caught in violent thoughts
Malignant phrases
Dangerous ideas
An apocalyptical destiny
Dreaming of a time that was

A false prophet
Speaking of causes
Issues
Others
Enemies
Blindly following dishonest Influencers
Over the edge
Into the abyss

Trapped
Lost, in a swirling maze
Of anger
Hate
Frustration
Slowly boiling,
Swelling
Then, exploding
In an eruption
Of death and destruction

Another Casualty

They move through the house in silence
Avoiding each other as much as they can
Barely speaking
Barely touching

He's changed, she said
A casualty of Trump
And the era Trump brought

Anger comes more easily
Words misunderstood
Intent attributed
Defensiveness
No ground given
Accusations
Slights
Power struggles
A sense of unfairness—inside him
Taking root and growing
Fed by an unrelenting assault—by select media

So, they avoid
Wrecking a relationship
That had so much hope and promise
One that was once strong and seemingly invincible

I had No Answer

(first in a sequence of three)

Sitting on the floor
Legs crossed
Thinking about the person to my left
Who was rolling a joint
Listening to a voice
Ranting words about
Pigs
Rights
Racism
War

Staring at terrified faces of Marine recruiters
A freshly rolled joint
Passed through my hands
To the person on my right

We were demonstrating
Against the Vietnam war
Recruitment for the war
Recruitment in this building
Whatever the reason
We demonstrated,
With our marijuana, music, and rhetoric

I sat
Surrounded by the dedicated—
As the not-so-dedicated looked on
Waiting to see what would happen

This is when I saw her
She was cashing a check
I got up
Approached her
My shaggy hair and all
I smiled
Put on the charm
She asked,
What I knew of the history of Vietnam
Of the French involvement
American involvement
Chinese involvement
I had no answer

She asked,
If I knew what it was like to be there
To fight in a war
To kill or be killed
I had no answer

I listened,
As she told me about her husband
Who enlisted at age eighteen
And died one year later
Fighting for what he believed

I felt small
Very small
I had no answer

Fate

(second in the sequence of three)

Standing in the night breeze
With tears in his eyes
Listening to drums
Beat rhythmically, his demise

Standing in a trench
Wounded and lost
A soldier of war
Which had much cost

Tell me, my father,
Where do I go
I'm only nineteen
Do you wish it so

Silently looking up
Beginning to pray
But the wind carries a bullet
Killing what he had to say.

Trying to Recover

(third in the sequence of three)

Rushing through the cold
Huddling
Hurrying

The wind,
Making it difficult to breathe
Stopping
Reading a poster
Talking about feeling alone

Snow resting on your jacket
Melting on your face
Camouflaging tears
Staring into your eyes

Feeling your hand squeezing mine
Inside my jacket pocket
Your loneliness
Your yearning
Not feeling the wind
Nor the rain

Trapped

He asked,
Who am I?
What do I regret?
What would I like to forget?
What have I done?
What have I become?
What would I like to change?
If I had the power to go back and rearrange?
What could I have been?
As I search within?
What would I like to be?
If I could set myself free?

His Changing State of Mind

It's like he's waiting
For someone to come,
For something to do,
For somewhere to go,
Without the excitement of anticipation,
Without the imaginative wonder and joy of what will be,
Of what could be.

It's like he's going through the motions,
Hoping, waiting
For something to change
Fleeting moments of happiness occasionally awake
Coming and going quickly—temporary spikes bringing joy
Then recede to a resting place
Waiting to be unearthed—dislodged, released

He wonders—
Is it age?
Physical decline?
Aches?
Pains?
Limitations?
Tiredness?
Frustration?
Disappointment?

Continual emotional bombardments
Dragging him down—into a hole.
A pit he wants to climb out of
To extricate himself from
A state of mind to change
That needs to change—
Before it grows
And becomes perpetual despair

What is He Becoming?

He's become rote, memorized, routine
Devoid of passion
Glimmers of hope, trying to emerge
Embers trying to burn stronger
Held back, by what?
You, life, the world, himself?

He looked inside, searching for an answer—any answer
Holding a mirror to himself
Seeing the reflection—who he is at this moment.

Not wanting it to take over
To trap him, define him
To dominate and control what he feels
What he does and how he does it
Not wanting it to be the lasting expression
Of what he is becoming

Lost Soul

Having everything owned
But nothing wanted
Everything used
But nothing enjoyed
Filling an insatiable appetite for possessions
Trying to fill an accepted void
It must be sad living alone
With no one to love but money

Loneliness

He stands alone
Naked to the world
Lifting his head to the skies
Spreading his arms to the sun
Begging not touch nor love
Just wanting someone
To join him in his thoughts
As brief as they may be
He so desperately needs that companionship

And the island of rock
Inevitably will turn to sand
Only to be washed away

You had the Power

You had the power the whole time
In your hands and still do
Regardless of age
To change, to overcome
Rather than succumb

To be successful, regardless of
Money, power
Title, influence
Contacts, breaks
Luck or likes

You complain about how difficult, how unfair,
What was or a lack of
You sit around
Waiting, evading
Contemplating
Maybe hating
Putting off
Avoiding

You had the power the whole time to use your talents,
To contribute,
And still do.
Wasting the opportunity God has given you—

To make your life meaningful
And purposeful
Which would make your life a success

Saint Nancy

Looking out the window
Seeing a fallen body—
Surrounded by children
Stunned
Not knowing what to do

Her neighbors,
Stuck
Not moving
Staring
At the fallen body
Pulling children away

Watching a circle
Edging back
Surrounding the man
Motionless and dead

Running to her bed
Grabbing her only blanket
Racing to the road
Where death lay

Kneeling beside the man
Blanketing his face and body
Clasping her hands to pray

Returning home
Calling the police
Who take the body away
And her only blanket

This is who she was
They say.

On the day of her funeral
Many came to mourn
And the priest called her
Saint Nancy
Whose mind was torn apart
By grief
When her two young children accidentally died

Captain John

Captain John docked his ship
And said farewell to his crew
I am leaving
I am leaving
I am leaving the sea
To try something new

With a hat in his hand
And a tear in his eye
He turned his back and walked
Stay a while
Stay a while
Stay a while, we hailed
Stay a while and talk

He didn't turn around
We didn't think he would
He just kept on walking
Kept on walking
Knowing he never could

We stayed aboard his lonely ship
Hoping his return
We drank and hailed
Prayed and wailed
Each taking a turn

He was a sailor
Sixty years at sea
He existed for all the world
But none so adoringly as me
For I was like his son
Born to him
On a dark port street
Drunk and mad
And awfully glad
He took me in
Making us complete

For thirty years
His ship was my mother
It nursed me and loved me
And I wished no other

Last night he took me aside
And told me of his pain
Of a world he knew existed
A disease he couldn't contain

Father, I cried in my sadness
You cannot die on me
Please! Please!
Please stay
And fight it on the sea
No,
No, my son came his answer
Softly he said
It's cancer

Captain John docked his ship
And said farewell to his crew
I am leaving
I am leaving the sea
To try something new
He didn't turn around
We didn't think he would
He just kept on walking
Kept on walking
Knowing he never could

Sigmund Freud

He wouldn't stop
To accept
As truth,
Assumptions
Of old-world medicine
Or
Take as fact
Thoughts
He could not see

He only asked why
Over and over
Till he could believe
That what he thought
But could not see
Was the cause
Of his doubts
And miseries

Skippy

He was my dog
Wagging tail
Happy bark
Always greeting
Always playing
Always there with loving eyes
Always displaying empathy
Always understanding and accepting

He died,
Running from July 4th firecrackers

He went insane
There was nothing we could do to help
He bolted through a screen door
And fled
And
Days later
We found him dead

The Counselor

You will bring your doubts
I will bring my ear
Together we'll create the strength
To eliminate this fear
That has boggled up your mind
And brought you here

Temporary Reprieve

He reached for happiness
And came up with sand
Turned mud
Hardening in his hand.

He washed off the mud
Cleaning away his fears
Watching it slowly drip
Along with his tears

This is when she touched his cheek
And kissed his hardened hand
But now she sleeps
And he sits near
Trying to understand
Why he's still scraping at his hand

Self-Abasement

He looked into a painting
And,
Saw his life
Spill before him
In the colors, hues, tints, and shades
Of gray and black

The paint slowly
Dripped to the floor
In an endless vision
Of disintegration

Freeing Himself

His mind fired up,
Rambling,
Finding places to set ablaze.
A whirling dervish of thoughts, emotions, energy
Caught up in a dance,
Worries, concerns, frustrations, sadness
Slights to sensitivities that hurt

Logic, understanding, rational thoughts, acceptance,
Can explain—can try to dismiss
But intense thoughts and emotions prevailed
Continuing their assault, growing stronger,
Penetrating,
Not letting go,
He needed an outlet,
A place to go,
A way to escape
Out of his mind,
Out of his body,
Out of his system—
Generating intense restlessness.

He began to speak—
Rambling words.
Letting it flow, letting it go

Loosening the binds, escaping the trap, liberation,
Finally!
He set himself free.
Enabling him to release, relax, let go,
To calm the mind and body,
Putting it all into a box of perspective
A miraculous transference
This act of freeing him from himself

Waiting Hopelessly

The telephone rings in silence
On the bare wall
In a white kitchen
Where a sign hangs
Bless this home

Sitting in a chair
Staring at the wall
She sits
Hands folded
Mind dull
Heart beating
Time has become endless

Undue Influence

She asked,
Is it OK to try just once?
A protective feeling overcame him
It didn't seem right
He was doing it for years—she had never
It wasn't bad for him
It might be for her
I trust you, she said
Just this once

He opened the drawer
Withdrew an ounce of marijuana and Zig Zag papers
He pulled out two sheets
Licked one of the gummed ends and stuck them together.
He felt her anticipation.

After creasing the paper
He placed the marijuana into the fold
His thumbs rolled upward
Leaving only the gummed end showing.
His tongue wet the end
His fingers pressed the joint into shape
Into his mouth for the final twist.
He asked,
Are you sure?

Yes, was her reply
Joint went to mouth
Match to joint
He inhaled
She followed his instructions.

The next day she asked,
Is it safe to do two days in a row?

Spiraling Downward

I see it all around,
Driven by anger
Feeding hate
Playing into fears
Us vs them
Unleashed, by people with agendas
Amplified, by some with good hearts
Who don't realize
Don't know
Or don't care
Throwing fuel on a fire
Making it grow
Making it glow
Making it worse
Making the world hotter

I see people,
Dancing around flames
Grabbing sticks
Lighting more fires
Spreading anger, hate, fear
Burning to the ground our faith,
In our country, people, the future

Making it difficult for growth
To emerge from ashes
For mercy and love to prevail
Dousing flames, diminishing fires
That will never fully extinguish
But can—more easily—be contained

Who can reverse this downward spiral?
Who can save us from ourselves?

Politicians at Their Worst

Tireless smiles
Zealously pursuing success
Playing games of competence
Each more worthy than the other

They slander and slit comrades
In the name of honest pursuit
Turning their office
Into a pigsty
Sleeping in filthy lies
Breathing blasphemous air
Rolling around in hypocrisy
Believing they are just.
Just what?

Charisma

He was stubborn
His strength adored
His honor respected
His courage admired
His perseverance envied
He was a good friend
A bad enemy

People
Followed him blindly,
His stubbornness
Until it was directed toward them.
How horribly dogmatic
He now became

They found,
He, like them
Did not see very well

Is It His Time?

What is that you say
This is the day?
Are you sure your news is just?
This is the man to trust?

That
He rides the wind
On a lovely song
Of a rainbow world
Where there is no wrong?

And yesterday he died?

An Idea

They found it floating effortlessly
In an ocean of time
It contained a note
Scribbled on a piece of paper
A few words of well-meaning
Which, when read
Meant nonsense
To those who read it

It was not their language
Not their time
Not their inclination
Not their destiny

The End

She fought,
Struggling against defeat
She thought,
Trying to make ends meet
Falling fast
And furthermore
She stopped,
To realize the score
She gave up,
Not living anymore

Suffering a Loss

He wandered
Lost in a daze
Mostly at night
Seeing things, he had never seen before
Feeling lost
Looking for her—himself
Knowing she couldn't be found

Burden

He walked through an open door
Across a busy street
Onto an open lot

He dropped to his knees
Leaned against a tree
Sighed
And stared at the ground

An ant crawled from beneath a rock
Carrying a morsel of food,
Twice its size.

He watched the ant struggle
With its heavy load
And began thinking of her

He fell asleep
Dreaming that she was by his side.

Misplaced Anger

He was angry with her
For leaving him
When he needed her most

He lashed out at the world
Spewing sarcasm and cynicism
Wherever he went.

He was angry
But never with himself

Alone in Sadness

His sadness is a voyage
To places he has never been
And to those he wishes to forget.

He drifts effortlessly into the past
And slowly tumbles into old haunts
Those memories,
Where a lifetime could be spent
Forcing numbness
Hopelessness.
Then he jolts
Into the unknown
Imagining what could be

He has no control
Of where it takes him
Only strength to endure

He is alone in his sadness
With no safe harbor
Letting no one in
Letting no one know

Now It's Real

He talked of times
When sadness
Was what others spoke of

It was theirs—not his
It was an idea—not a feeling
It was understood—not felt
It was interesting—not absorbing
It was many things but not sad

Now it is his sadness
It is felt
It hurts
It's his
And It's real

Happiness

Happiness,
That glorious moment of elation
That remarkable moment of joy
Comes increasingly less often.
Sadness,
Frequently more persistent—
Defining his new norm.

Remnants from an Acid Trip

He is adrift on a raft
In his ocean of a mind
The sun is hot
The water salty
There is no land in sight
It's a voyage
An experience

He wants to scream
To jump out of himself
And shake himself back
To wherever he was before
He is scared
That it may never end.

Thoughts of Suicide

He's splitting into two people
One, grasping for life
Not knowing where to go
Or how to get there
The other, reaching for death
Knowing how, but not why

His thoughts spin
Mind frays
Body weakens
Tiredness dictates
Dreams melt away—evaporate
Sadness envelopes

He endures as he has before
Knowing,
When it is over
He will be stronger.

Battles give strength,
Understanding,
Tools he can use
When these feelings return

Returning Home

With Intensifying emotions
Chaotic thoughts
And Floundering hands
His inability stands
Return he must,
To the comforts of home
Where he can begin again

Social Anxiety

Go ahead
Stare out the window
It's daylight
No one can see inside
The sun reflects all

Watch the people
The person
Just curious
Go ahead
Stare out the window
Go ahead
Try to go outside

Being Self-Conscious

Self-consciousness about
What others think
How he will be perceived
Holds him back—
Often preventing him from taking
That leap of faith
To pursue
What he feels
God designed him to do

His Mind

His mind
Continually racing
Jumping all over
Often roaming—imagining
Needing focus to be productive
Something
To latch on to
Throw himself into
Eventually,
Exhausting itself
Bringing tiredness
Then shutting down

Perfection

They sought perfection
Only to trap themselves
Unable to move forward
Held back
Stuck
Frustrated
Emotionally drained
By an impossible expectation
Of perfection
Of themselves
Of others

Hesitancy

Tenderly they look
Longing to touch
So gently they speak
Afraid of words
Fearing their pasts
Which are far behind

Give them time
Give them time

Approaching the End of Life on Earth

Approaching the End

Once, there were endless possibilities
Time, not an issue
Energy, not a problem
Always looking forward
At what could be
Life an open field

Now, looking back
At what was
Recalling, recollecting, remembering, reflecting

Time, once infinite
Now, limited
A precious resource that is running out

It can't be held off
A slow-moving fog
Limiting sight
Diminishing capability
Longing for what was
Suppressing

The end grows closer
The journey—almost over
The path—almost complete
Time—almost gone

Brief moments arise
Then, slowly recede
Oh, what this does to
The mind, body, and spirit

When did it start?
When did the feeling begin?
It doesn't make a difference—
It's here—and here to stay—
The new normal to live with
Adjust to

Does acceptance mean capitulation?
or the reality that a transition has begun?

Coming to Terms with What Will Be

As I grow older
The closer I come to terms
With my eventual demise,
The closer I come to seeing
In my mind's eye.
What I Feel
What I need
How it will be

It's disturbing,
This image,
These thoughts.

When did this start?
Was there a trigger?
A natural progression?
Maybe both?

Regardless,
It has found a resting place
A home,
Rearing its ugly head—
At times taking over

Thoughts of Dying

It's difficult leaving
A place you like
For another.
One foot here
The horizon there
Giving up something you know
Have gotten used to
Comfortable with
For the unknown
The promise of what could be.

It's inevitable,
Dying comes
Sometimes suddenly—
Unwelcomed
Sometimes longed for—
The final relief

Belief in Heaven
Brings comfort
Regardless,
You move on
Have no choice
Praying for the best

What's Comes Next

What of the next world?
The unknown
What God promised
Jesus said exists
Something to hold on to
Hope for
Believe in

A new world
A new possibility
A new beginning
A new life
A rebirth
A new womb to climb from
A new existence to enter

Sleep Used to Be

A mystery
I tried to catch
Each night

Waiting,
Wanting to see
Its approach

With blinding speed
It inevitably
Surrounded me
Gently
Swayed me
Soothingly caressed me

Its secret
Remained a mystery
Conquering
Each night
And I not knowing
Till
It released me
In the morning

Sleep Now

I awake to the need, AGAIN.
Third time tonight.
I stumble to the bathroom.
Hand on the wall.
Steadying myself around the corner.
Sleep slowly drains,
as I wait for the flow to begin—I wait.

I trudge back to bed.
My mind begins to unleash itself.
Thoughts sprouting, on their own.
I lay down.

My brother Jay in a nursing home.
Sister Joan in assisted living.
Another brother, Gene,
Dealing with cancer.
Twenty-seven years now.
Can't believe he has suffered so and survived.
Mom, Dad
May they rest in peace.
Their dying days.
Children: Kevin, Katie.
Does the worry ever stop?
Grandkids: David, Libby.
They bring such joy.

Moments of love, anger, triumph, disappointment, life.
What the future will bring.
God, Jesus.
Hitting my three hybrid, pickleball, bike paths
My body moves this way,
then that way.
Restlessness grows, the mind flows.

Diane lying next to me.
Her slow breathing.
A steady rhythm.
Forty-seven years.
Has it been that long?
Time flies.
Tons of memories flood in about her, us, our life.

My mind now unleashed—
Cascades easily
Pouring endlessly.
No door remains unlocked.
No rabbit holes remain unexplored.
It's now 4:00 AM.
Too much on my mind, as it races.

My body moving, independently.
Legs, arms, head, flailing about
In turbulent agitation
Matching my thoughts.

Calm abandons.
Quits, departs, disappears.
Sleep evaporates.
The battle is lost.

Anxiety overtakes.
My inescapable adversary has invaded once more,
Again prevails—inevitable acceptance.
Time to get up.
To read, settle the mind, stop the flow.
Calm the restlessness.
Put out the mental fire.

As the Door Slowly Closes

As the door slowly closes and
The final lap begins
I think,
Enjoy moments
Exploit interests
Find ways to use my God-given talents
Especially in support of others
Be giving
Do good
Develop my soul

Live what life I can
Appreciate the opportunities God gives me
And
Never lose belief
Never lose faith
That a new door will open
That God doesn't abandon.

One View of Death

Death is God's way of saying
It's time to move on to the next phase

As I write this
I'm still alive
So, I guess
God is not
Finished with me yet

Moving On

Moving on from Loneliness

Reach out to others
Help those in need
Guide those who fear
Respond, believe, have faith
Grow, develop, learn

For time ceases in lonely caverns
Where memories bring pain
Where joy fades
Dreams die
And the future
Brings little hope and peace

Don't Give Up

Witness the sights
Hear the sounds
Join the voices
On the merry-go-round

Lose your age
Remember the past
Grab a horse and ride
Real fast

It's not as difficult
As it might appear
The time has come
So, jump on here

Throw your head back
Grab the bar
Lean over the railing
Reach for a star

A Protective Wall

Finding purpose—
In things
Big and small
Important and unimportant
Noticed and unnoticed

Sometimes coming
In moments of
Joy
In moments of
Contentment
Frequently, when fully engaged
Using your giftedness
Lost in a zone
In a flow
Where an hour feels like a minute

Seek out those moments
Save them
Bank them
Draw upon them
Use them
As a protective wall
To balance
Those thoughts

That can
Tear you apart
Tear you down
Emotionally
Physically
Bringing darkness and despair

We Can

We can be a beacon
As tiny as our footprints might be
Of hope, promise, goodness
To help stem the tide
Of the rising anger, hate, pain, and sickness
That is all around
Rather than
Sit in silence and ignore,
Or lash out in hate and violence

We can,
Let love, mercy, and God guide us
In our actions
In our words

We can,
Reach out and let Him in
To give peace of mind and a calm heart

We can,
Enjoy the good moments that come along
Despite all the disappointments and frustrations

We can,
Use the pain to develop our souls

And
Allow God to shine a light
So, things are more clearly seen

Momentum

When life appeared bleakest
When I was wallowing
Feeling sorry for myself
Trapped in stagnation
Sluggish
Listless
Producing no movement
A self-imposed prison

At those moments,
When lethargy took over mind and body
I forced myself
To become involved—
To create energy—
Momentum

I learned,
A body at rest stays at rest
A body in motion stays in motion
I learned,
Behavior precedes emotion.
If I get active and involved,
Positive energy will begin to flow.
Changing everything
And it did

God

Spending Time with God

Quietly, I sit
Listening to God work miracles
In my mind

Hand in hand
We move
His spirit, flowing over me
Through me
Comforting
Calming
Assuring
Feeling His presence

I'm not alone
I'm grounded
Accepted for who I am
What I've done
And, failed to do

I pour out all that is buried inside
That needs expression
Needs to be released
Visits I periodically make

Being accepted—
By God—
Is a wonderful feeling

There Comes a Time

There comes a time when we confront ourselves
Our inadequacies—
The life we have led and
Still have left to live
For me,
It is often late at night
As I lay in bed
Unable to sleep

All is quiet,
Silence
Darkness
No distractions
No escape
I lay myself bare

It is a pit, difficult to climb out of
As I claw away, sinking deeper—
But also, a springboard
To new ways, new determinations, new awareness,
Growth, development
Sometimes crying out as I confront myself
This is when I pray,
For insight, strength, comfort, help, forgiveness, guidance

God never lets me down—
He never seems to be very far away
He's always with me on these journeys

Always There

He is always there
Quiet
Supportive
Encouraging
As I listen
Learn
Teaching me the
Wonderment of life
Of living
Of giving

He is always there
Behind me
Next to me
Within me

Naivete

The fool to be
Is the fool, not I
Is the fool not I to be
A fool I was
To blind I was
That a fool I was destined to be
Until,
He set me free

He Is

He is,
The expression of God
Demonstrating His love, mercy, and grace
Not hate, anger, and fear

Reaching out to those who are
Hurting, in pain, hopeless, helpless, in need

Confronting hypocrisy
Of religious leaders
And those with false authority
Who distort God for their own benefit, glory, power
Intoxicating influence

Assuring people of eternal life in heaven
Showing them the path to get there
Being an example—
Someone to emulate—
Showing the way to live
Teaching, educating
Providing hope and comfort
When all else feels lost

Why are so many
Turning a blind eye—losing their way?

Feeling Connected

I shed tears in sadness—
I feel alone.
I smile in gladness—
I feel happy.
I rage in madness—
I feel angered.
I ache in pain—
I feel hurt.
I take risks in doubt—
I feel fear.
I touch in warmth—
I feel love.
I write poems in solitude—
I feel relief.
I speak with God in need
I feel connected

Acknowledgments

I want to express appreciation to Ed Edelson, Blaine Greenfield, Nancy Anne Miller, Steve Mocko (former college English professor who helped turn my life around), Ed Poff, Glenn Rifkin, Fred Sievert, and Tommy Thomas who all graciously read early versions of the manuscript and provided invaluable feedback, both positive and negative, that helped shape the final version of this book.

I would also like to give a special thank you to the team at Wipf and Stock Publishers for their support and excellent work.

About the Author

Steve M. Darter has had a distinguished career as a consultant, author, and educator. For almost fifty years he has counseled people ranging from troubled teenagers to CEOs of Fortune 500 corporations on work, career, and life issues. He is the retired president of People Management Northeast. Aside from *Inside My Mind*, Steve has authored *Lessons from Life: Four Keys to Living with More Meaning Purpose and Success* which was ranked by one media company as the #1 "Profound Book About Finding Yourself" and *Managing Yourself Managing Others: Learn How to Improve Effectiveness, Productivity, and Work Satisfaction*. During his long career, Steve has interviewed and evaluated close to five thousand people and has taught courses on career counseling and managing to strengths in two graduate schools.

Steve was born and raised on Long Island, spent most of his professional life in the Hartford, Connecticut area, and now lives in New Jersey to be near his grandkids. He and his wife, Diane, are huge UConn basketball fans, both men and women.

For more information on Steve or to contact him
www.StevenDarter.com
www.PeoplemanagementSMD.com

www.ingramcontent.com/pod-product-compliance
Lightning Source LLC
Chambersburg PA
CBHW071723090426
42738CB00009B/1858